HOW TO
MAKE WORRY
WORK FOR YOU

HOW TO MAKE WORRY WORK FOR YOU

SIMPLE AND PRACTICAL LESSONS ON HOW TO BE HAPPY

CRAIG B. MARDUS, Ph.D.

WARNER BOOKS

A Time Warner Company

Warner Books, Inc., 1271 Avenue of the Americas,
New York, NY 10020
W A Time Warner Company

Printed in the United States of America
First Printing: June 1995
10 9 8 7 6 5 4 3 2 1

Library of Congress Cataloging-in-Publication Data

Mardus, Craig B.
  How to make worry work for you : simple and practical lessons on
how to be happy / Craig B. Mardus.
      p.   cm.
  ISBN 0-446-51967-7
  1. Stress (Psychology)   2. Stress management.   3. Worry.
I. Title.
BF575.S75M336   1995
155.9'042—dc20   94-44962

Book design by Giorgetta Bell McRee

To my parents for encouraging my imagination.

Contents

CONTENTS

CONTENTS

Introduction

As most people do who grow up feeling troubled, I turned introspective to try to figure out why I had clouds over my head and tension in my body. In school my stomach got upset easily and I experienced headaches and nervousness. Even so, I thought I was a fun-loving little kid with a good imagination and sense of humor.

Much later I realized that I had a very sensitive nervous system. I reacted to other people and events in a magnified way, causing my body to suffer stress. This oversensitivity resulted in feelings of tension, depression, and an overall fear of living. A good day was a day when things around me went well. The days that did not go well, when things around me did not go well, produced profoundly harmful effects on my mind and body. Eventually too many of these bad days turned that fun-loving little kid into a negative, cynical, and angry adult. I covered up well in social settings but still wanted to know why I felt this way. All my self-grown theories and introspection just made a confusion of the whole mess. I continued to have my good days and my bad days . . . just reacting to life.

Then I got my wake-up call. It came at age thirty-two when I was diagnosed with cancer. I was lucky. It only took two operations and a year of recovery to be back in health. Since I was going to live, I decided then and there to deal with my fear of living. I already had my doctorate in counseling, but wasn't using it. I planned a self-study program in stress. I bought some computerized biofeedback instruments and used them to take a hard look at my autonomic nervous system—the place where fear and stress live.

All the current stress theories and research were pointing toward relaxation as the answer to stress, so I learned to relax my overly sensitive nervous system with the help of the biofeedback machines, which would show me when I was succeeding. It was hard to relax on command, staring at the cold computer screen. There was a force making it difficult for me to relax on cue. This was when I first started to understand the sabotage agenda the autonomic nervous system has for us when we try to control it. And even if I could relax for the machines, I certainly couldn't relax in the heat of a tense moment or when worrying about something. It seemed as though this force was acting on me, compelling me to worry or feel bad. I couldn't understand it.

Eventually the biofeedback machines slowly gave up the secrets of the autonomic nervous system to my watchful eyes, usually through mistakes I made while trying to relax. I discovered I was looking in the wrong place for the source of control. This book reveals the secrets that helped me turn a life of fear into a life of challenge and opportunity. The secrets that helped me reunite with that fun-loving little kid and let him play with life. The old ghosts still haunt me when things go wrong, but now I have a good plan to deal with them. You will too.

HOW TO
MAKE WORRY
WORK FOR YOU

Chapter 1

SHORTCUTS FOR NORMAL NUTS

*W*hen stress attacks us we either deal with it in an efficient manner, or we succumb. We automatically, unthinkingly reach for any one of an endless list of bad habits that act as a numbing agent for the pain of that overwhelming stress. The bad habits give us the illusion of control, but instead add guilt. The stress goes unchecked and forms a series of stress-related symptoms such as anxiety, depression, insomnia, anger, procrastination, difficulty in relaxing, feeling rushed, fear, and lowered self-esteem. This book explains how all these side effects of poor stress management come about and gives you simple, foolproof methods of overcoming them—NOW.

I call those people who experience the symptoms on this list "normal nuts" because to some extent we *all* experience this list as part of being human in today's world. This book is *not* designed for those suffering clinical psychological illnesses.

The shortcuts are the unique discoveries I have made about the autonomic nervous system (ANS), the place where stress lives. Using these discoveries shows us how to deal better with stress when it attacks, and so avoid succumbing to the bad habits for the illusion of control they bring. We will deal instead with real control, and that is why there is no chapter on habit control. The entire book *is* habit control.

Chapter 2

MY VIEW OF THE AUTONOMIC NERVOUS SYSTEM (ANS)

$\mathcal{T}$ he autonomic nervous system (ANS) is not under your control. It takes care of itself. It regulates the release of adrenaline, the stress response, worry, fear, anxiety, blood pressure, heart rate, nervous sweat, hand temperature, and about a million other functions that you don't even know exist. The ANS is designed to save your life and keep you alive. By comparison, the central nervous system (CNS) *is* under your control. You can move your muscles and thus your skeleton. You can walk, smile, scratch your head; it's easy.

What the ANS hates is when you try (read: fail) to control it. It loves to sabotage your attempts to defeat its purpose. For example, if I were to ask

3

you *not:* to blink, swallow, or think of a naked person of the opposite sex, guess what? You would do the opposite. If you have an upset child and you tell him to "sit in that chair and relax," he won't.

Biofeedback has taught us that with practice you *can* control some of the ANS functions, usually by teaching relaxation among other things. My experience, however, with biofeedback and the ANS has shown me a new way to control it by *not* controlling it. Be prepared in this book for some unique ways of using the ANS's loopholes.

Chapter 3

THE REAL PURPOSE OF ADRENALINE

$\mathcal{T}$ he main function of the ANS is to save your life. It does this with the automatic release of adrenaline into your bloodstream. It's a reflex, a response to danger. As a reflex it involves *no effort*. It's a no-brainer. It just happens. It is the fight-or-flight response that gets you ready to deal with any life-threatening emergency. It puts you into an ultrafast (beyond thinking) state of arousal to help you survive.

A simple example of this would be if you were in a New York City parking garage late at night, and a car backfired. You would be startled and jump. You didn't have to think about it, it just happened. Your heart will be beating faster, and your palms will be sweaty as you prepare for survival. As soon as you realize it was only a car (now you are thinking), you let the adrenaline go (stop releasing it), and start to feel better.

In our everyday life we rarely *need* to use this response. Perhaps a close call in traffic, when an elevator lurches, when we slip on ice, are scared by someone in a dark laundry room, or when an airplane shudders. Rarely do these events last for more than a few seconds. Our brain sees them for what they are and stops the heightened response from continuing. If it were a real survival situation (like combat) you would have loads of adrenaline to see you through. This type of extreme survival situation is rare for us today in a civilized world. When we lived in caves, every sound or change in our environment could have signaled impending death. It was a good response then. It was designed for a crueler world. We misuse that response today.

Let me take you through a simple ANS adrenaline response:

> *You're driving your car. Someone swerves in front of you. You feel pins and needles travel down your arms, your palms get a flash of sweat. You see things in slow motion, make*

the necessary steering, braking corrections, and get out of trouble. That might have taken ten seconds. Now *you feel nervous, scared, experience palpitations, trembling, dry throat, and difficulty breathing. These are the effects of residual adrenaline that wasn't used up in the ten seconds of active surviving. This feels bad. It didn't feel like anything during the ten seconds because you were too busy saving your life. Adrenaline protects you that way while you do the surviving. Once you've survived, you start feeling the adrenaline. It was never designed to be felt! You are supposed to be too busy.*

Whenever you release adrenaline improperly (as in worry, anxiety, fear), you experience its effects, and it feels bad. You're not absorbed in a survival situation so it feels the same as that excess adrenaline after the ten-second close call. We have become great misusers of our own adrenaline. This book addresses those misuses and shows you better ways to "misuse" it—ways that will make you feel good!

Chapter 4

USE (MISUSE) OF OTHER TIME ZONES

Our bodies live in the "now." By the now I mean right this instant. That is real. The now. Human beings differ from other mammals in that we were also given the gift of going into other time zones with our brain even though our body remains in the now. We are supposed to use this gift of being able to think of the future or past in a good way.

If used positively, this gift allows the future to be full of hopes, dreams, goals, aspirations, plans, and security. It allows the past to hold fond memories and nostalgic reminiscences. Just as we believe our nighttime dreams and feel the feelings that are part of their script when we are dreaming, we also feel those good feelings when we go into the future or past in a positive way. This gift makes our now even better for our bodies.

When we take this gift and misuse it, we make the future full of anxieties and worries ("What if _____?") and the past full of depression, anger, and resentment ("If only _____!"). This leads to negative feelings in our now bodies. Mark Twain once said, "I've had a great deal of catastrophes in my life, but luckily most of them never happened!" He was describing worry. We put our now bodies through hell when we misuse this gift of being able to go into the past or future. Thus when we go into another time zone, we release adrenaline and make the body feel bad (tense, depressed) in the now. We create nightmares instead of daydreams. We misuse the original design.

A cat only lives in the now. It doesn't sit there wondering if it's going to get the good cat food tomorrow. As an example, if a cat were to see another cat, it would release adrenaline (its tail would get *real* big and its fur would stand up) and prepare for battle. If the other cat runs out of sight and smell, that first cat doesn't sit there worrying about whether or not that cat will come back. Instead it starts licking its foot! It doesn't care. A young child before it learns how to worry acts the same.

While you read on, be aware that there are two ways to use (misuse) the gift.

Chapter 5

MYTHS OF RELAXATION—AND THE TRUTH

I have a lot of stress in my life." "I'm stressed out." "I have a very stressful job." I hear this a lot in my practice as a stress management consultant. If you ask the person what they want in the session, they'll say, "I want to learn some techniques so I can relax when I'm feeling stressed out at work." I respond by saying, "Oh, you want a miracle!" They smile and begin to realize the myth of relaxation.

The one thing relaxation wasn't designed to do was to get you relaxed *while* in the middle of stress. This Band-Aid approach to stress won't work. What it will do is create the mentality that "I need a drug to turn off this stress, now!" That creates the bad-habit and prescription-drug approach to stress.

Stress management is what you use when in the stress. And it works. Stress management is dynamic and is designed to get you through it. Stress management works on control issues, not relaxation. People who practice relaxation techniques and then see me are often confused as to how to use them. They don't have the time, luxury, or opportunity to leave the scene of a stress situation to do progressive relaxation, tai chi, yoga, meditation, autogenics, Clynes cycles, Benson's relaxation response, self-hypnosis, breath counting, biofeedback, or Stroebel's quieting reflex. When I suggest they take time out during the stress, they look at me while shaking their heads because they know it wouldn't be appropriate then.

Relaxation *is* very important. But *when* is it appropriate? It is in understanding the when of relaxation that will allow you to receive its full benefits.

Let yourself see relaxation as a vitamin pill. You take it at a time that *you* choose. You thus make it easy to successfully relax, and you give yourself permission to do it guilt-free. Relaxation is done in downtime. This way it gives you restorative rest and acts in a preventive, indirect way. If you relax once a day, it makes that day easier to handle. It gives you resilience, a stress hardiness. If you remove relaxation, you become irritable and stress-prone that day.

When you are under stress, you are in the middle of a problem. Even if you could duck out and get a massage, you'd feel guilty and tense and wouldn't let it relax you. The problem is not closed. What it needs is stress management.

This probably explains why there are no hot tubs in offices! The goal at work is not to be relaxed, but to be in control of your work. In the middle of a heated board meeting, one board member doesn't suggest to another that he go to the corporate gym and do a step class! It's not appropriate, nor would it work.

The old TV or movie stereotype of Al Capone getting a massage, haircut, and manicure, with half-naked babes around the office *while* he conducts business is not a realistic view of work. Neither is a guy selling real estate from his yacht.

Relaxing is an effort if you try to do it when you are experiencing stress. It becomes easier when you plan it in downtime for the refresher it is. The guilt-free condition required for relaxation means that you cannot be rushing to do it or telling yourself that you should be doing work or something else instead. That's the voice of guilt. That voice requires self-permission to take that time for you.

I see three types of relaxation: passive, active, and formal. Relaxation techniques represent the formal type. They are deliberate attempts to relax on purpose. They must be learned and practiced and may cause some anxiety, fear, or frustration at first. It's the hardest way of the three to relax because you are working against the ANS and trying to tell it what to do.

The other two ways are easier and avoid all that necessity to learn and practice, not to mention avoiding the problem of trying to control the ANS!

Passive and active relaxation both involve activities to focus on. That takes away the direct ANS control. Some examples of passive relaxation: reading, napping, listening to music, petting the cat, watching a movie, sitting by a fireplace, knitting. You do the activity in guilt-free, planned downtime—and you have no choice but to get relaxed. It's easy.

Active forms of relaxation might include sports, hobbies, dancing, and exercise. You do the activity and you feel relaxed.

Most sessions in relaxation training that I do involve getting people in touch with their passive and active forms of relaxation, and helping them find guilt-free time in their busy lifestyle.

Relaxation's preventive (vitamin pill) use for stress can even be used in advance. Say it was 2:00 P.M. Friday, and you were about to see a client who always pushes your stress button; you might not get as upset if you knew you were going to have a great tennis game at 6:00!

Remember, when you try to relax during stress, your ANS will fight your attempt to relax with more power than you have. If you plan relaxation during downtime that you create for yourself, there are no control issues going on, so your ANS is not involved and it becomes easier for you to relax.

In this book there are many models to help you use stress management. But please remember: don't try to use relaxation for stress management; it won't work and will only frustrate you.

Chapter 6

PHANTOM ADRENALINE: NEGATIVE MISUSE

*W*orrying is when you use your mind to go into the future and fantasize trouble. You leave a perfectly good now and release adrenaline (you get tense, stressed, pressured) because you let your mind convince your body that you are really in that bad situation. You usually worry about something because you fear that it might happen, and that it would make you feel stressed if it did indeed happen. The thinking alone makes you instantly feel the stress in a perfectly good now body. The irony is you get the bad physical effect without even having to experience the bad reality!

HOW TO MAKE WORRY WORK FOR YOU

*If you were sitting in a chair at home wor-
rying about appearing in traffic court next
week, your body would probably be feeling as
it would if you were in traffic court and things
were going badly. You released adrenaline for
a fantasy. I call this "phantom adrenaline,"
just as phantom pain is real pain from a part
of the body that isn't there anymore. It still
hurts! This is real adrenaline being released by
a worry (a stress fantasy) and the body feels bad
in the now where nothing is really happening.*

It's important to differentiate between thinking
and worrying, because some of you are probably
saying it's okay to worry about certain things.
Here's the difference: If you were worrying about
something for three days and one morning in the
shower you realized a solution to your worries . . .
that's thinking. You solved a problem. That's what
thinking and the brain are for. Call it thinking instead of worrying, and label it okay. If someone
says, "Stop worrying about that," tell them you're
not worrying, you're thinking. I call this "psycho-
semantics"—the psychological power of words on
our attitude. If, however, you are thinking about
how to change your mother-in-law, or how to

solve the Mideast crisis, you can *live* in the shower and never find a solution. That's worrying. You have no control over that stuff. That's only going to hurt you.

Worrying is the prime misuse of the stress response. That is why this book exists. There is no life-threatening event, yet the worry produces adrenaline just as easily as if it were there. Worry uses the same reflexive, effortless mechanism as the real stress response (as in combat).

You don't have to practice worrying because it fools the body with a stress fantasy, and unless the body is in a hot tub or on vacation, it will feel bad instantly and effortlessly from the worry.

When you feel the tension and pressure of the worry, you usually only want relief, relaxation, and peace. But that's the one thing that the autonomic nervous system won't let you have because relaxation doesn't work when you are producing adrenaline. Your attempt at relaxation then usually causes feelings of frustration, which puts you in a classic no-win situation. Remember that relaxation is not an effortless reflex. It is not part of the survival response. It is learned and practiced, and only works when there is no stress (control issues).

Adrenaline was designed to be used up. It hates

to be calmed down. That only causes frustration. That is why people use bad habits and drugs to attempt to instantly calm the tense body caused by the reflex action of phantom adrenaline. Only an IV of morphine or a bullet can get rid of the power of adrenaline instantly!

Chapter 7

PHANTOM EXCITEMENT: POSITIVE MISUSE NO. 1

$\mathcal{T}$ his is the chapter where you will learn to get rid of worry in one second without effort. The solution is simple:

> *Just think of a* very exciting thought *the next time you are worrying. A smile will come over your face, and you will feel* good *in one second, effortlessly.*

I've used this technique (call it the Mardus Maneuver if you like) on thousands of worriers with great success. I did find, however, that it is not enough to just tell you the secret. People want to know why it works, so let me explain all about it.

It all started with skydiving. By interviewing

people who have decided they wanted to skydive, I came across an interesting bit of information about the autonomic nervous system and adrenaline. Let me walk you through a skydive experience.

> *You decide you want to skydive. You take the ground course in the morning, pay the fee, and before you know it, you're standing in front of an open plane door thousands of feet in the air. How do you think you feel? The correct answer for a human being is* scared to death, *okay? You don't want to feel scared, it just happens, effortlessly. Then you jump, full of fear and terror. Once you pull the ripcord, do you think you will feel relaxed or exhilarated one second afterward? The correct answer is ex-hilarated. Do you ask to feel exhilarated, or does it just happen? It just happens, effortlessly. What happened to the fear, terror, and scared-to-death feelings? They are G-O-N-E! You don't even wonder where they went because you feel too good being exhilarated.*

To recap: you went from the world's worst feeling to the world's best feeling in one second, effort-lessly!

Your ANS showed you its weak link, but until now it hasn't been applied to stress management. If you miniaturize that skydive down to one of your worries, and apply the same principle, the same effect can happen to you. Since we know it works well for the worst-case scenario, it has to work for your worry as well.

Before I run you through a worry, let me explain exactly what happened when that chute opened. When you stood in that doorway and then jumped, you were pumping large quantities of adrenaline. There is no way you could relax in that doorway. Gandhi couldn't relax in *that* doorway! As you were falling, you were in a classic out-of-control scenario. That's what makes the adrenaline feel bad (tension and panic). In a later chapter on the two types of control, I define stress as "people and things *not* going your way." Falling in the air your first time skydiving definitely qualifies as stress. But when you open the chute, *you gain complete control* so you *relabel* that bad adrenaline as good adrenaline. The relabeling process takes less than one second and is effortless. As you take hold of the excitement (exhilaration) you instantly let go of the fear. You can't hold both together. Since you are not trying to get rid of the adrenaline, you are *not* fighting the ANS. You are letting it do what it likes to do best . . . produce even more adrenaline, but this time it is good adrenaline.

If you were relaxed now, and I had you think of an exciting thought, you would probably feel excited instantly. This I call "phantom excitement," and is positive misuse No. 1 of the stress response. You produced adrenaline with an excitement fantasy, and your body feels: invigorated, excited, exhilarated, tingly, bubbly, pumped, surged, open, psyched, ready, and *alive*. This is what good adrenaline feels like. It's not stress, and it's not relaxation. It's good stress. It is exactly as powerful as phantom adrenaline or real adrenaline. It's really all the same adrenaline.

Now, let me walk you through a worry.

Think about something you usually worry about. Something not going your way. Something, at this point, out of your control. Feel the instant tension the release of phantom adrenaline creates in your now body. Try to relax it away. Any success? Maybe you got lucky and were able to let the tension go? Maybe you couldn't and got even more upset? If you still have the tension, think about some-

thing really exciting: great sex, winning the lottery, doing a 360 on skis, your parachute just opening, a hole in one, acing your tennis serve, great sex again! There's probably a smile on your face now, and the worry's G-O-N-E! You feel good. Check it out.

See if you have any of the alive feelings in your body. Most people have a close relationship with the tightness and tension in their body. They can describe it in detail when they are stressed. If these people can relax, some of them can describe their relaxed feeling, but most just say "lack of tension." They describe it in negative stress terms. They are not as deeply sensitive and in touch with what re-laxation is. Relaxation is a state of being quiet, calm, loose, peaceful, serene, settled. On the other hand, when these people get excited, or when they switch from tension (worry) to excitement, they still *think* (not feel) they are tight even though there is a smile on their face and they tell you they feel "good." They're just not attuned enough to recognize excitement in their life. They are stuck in the "tense . . . not tense" binary state. They need to get back in touch with their ability to feel alive.

Connect the "alive," "changed" excitement feeling with the smile and good feeling, instead of "I'm not relaxed."

> *Let's look at the two elements either of which is necessary to create an exciting thought and feeling (phantom excitement): high physical risk or great sex. We're not interested in going to the beach here. That's relaxation. It won't work. These two elements should be a fantasy, not connected to reality. A fantasy is so terrific it will probably never happen in your life. That's what makes it a great escape from worry. The subject of your worry will probably never happen either! (Remember that Mark Twain quote?)*

When you are worrying, it is a negative fantasy. You're watching a horror movie and are handcuffed to the seat. You feel bad and stuck. You're producing phantom adrenaline. When you think that exciting thought, you instantly transport to another movie where you are watching a positive fantasy where you have complete control. You are the producer, the director, and the star. This is a shift from bad to good adrenaline. It is really a shift from no control to total control, which relabels the bad adrenaline good. Read that again.

The worry is G-O-N-E, and you're happy. Those two elements of excitement can be remembered easily with these two words: risky or risqué. High adventure or great sex with anyone you want. I'm talking Mel Gibson and Sharon Stone here!

You're really curing one fantasy with another. You're using one misuse to cure another misuse of the life-saving stress response. It's not just an escape. The Mardus Maneuver works better and better with bigger and bigger worries. We know this because it always works when your parachute opens! (The chapter on fear and risk will tell you how to enjoy the first part of that skydive jump.)

Using excitement to cure worry is like using fire to fight fire. Using relaxation to cure worry is like throwing gasoline on fire. It's like stopping a charging bull by standing in front of it.

It's really important now to discuss what happens fairly quickly after an exciting thought and feeling. It's an interesting phenomenon that I call "Miller Time," as in the beer commercial. There is a relaxation that has to occur after excitement. It is automatic. It always happens. Every time you ever got excited in life (as a child or yesterday), you followed it with relaxation. This Miller Time phenomenon happens with this worry technique as well. You'll get excited, lose the worry, and then start relaxing automatically very soon afterward. It's as though the excitement were used as a catalyst to bring you from worry to relaxation (Miller Time) indirectly. That would make sense since it can't be done directly through normal ANS channels.

Thus you are controlling the ANS by *not* controlling it. You are using its ability to *not* know the difference between reality and fantasy to help you. (You believe all your dreams.) You are applying that skydiving loophole to worry and succeeding effortlessly.

Worry will now be a good thing for you because it just means you've got the adrenaline, and now it's time to get excited and then calm (Miller Time).

I like the image of taking a swan dive into excitement, yelling "Geronimo" on the way down! See worry as the steps leading to a high-diving platform. It's tense climbing to that height, but then you get to take that swan dive into great excitement. The higher the steps, the better the dive. Worry is now foreplay to excitement!

To add credibility to the skydive experience,

look at a football player running a touchdown play. He's got fear when he sees two large tackles in front of him, but when he gets past them and across that touchdown line, he explodes with exhilaration. The best sex people have is after a fight or funeral. You can see this no-control to total-control phenomenon everywhere.

Now you can use it for worry, fear, and anxiety.

Chapter 8

FAILED EXCITEMENT:
POSITIVE MISUSE NO. 2

T here is another interesting misuse of the stress
response that can be employed to help you relax
without the feeling of *trying* that relaxation techniques usually have. I call it "failed excitement."
This method gets you relaxed by *not* relaxing or
even trying to. Instead you are trying to get excited
and failing. Don't get hung up with the word "fail"
here—this is a good, planned fail!

The word "try" usually implies that something
is not going to work, that it will fail instead. At
AA meetings they'll tell you that if you're trying,
you're lying. You have to just do it. I'm going to
capitalize on the guaranteed failing aspect of trying
with this third misuse (positive misuse No. 2).

Let's do an example.

CRAIG B. MARDUS, PH.D.

If you're in your thirties or older, perhaps you can remember a person you dated in high school who was really exciting. Maybe five years later if you had thought of that person, you would have felt excited (phantom excitement). But maybe ten years later, when you thought of that same person, you didn't get excited anymore. What did you get? The answer is relaxed. It's now just a nice memory, calming and peaceful. You used up the excitement and are left with relaxation.

Some of you when asked to think of something exciting when worrying (in the last chapter) found that the worry disappeared (G-O-N-E), but you didn't feel that alive, exhilarated feeling. In that case you went right into failed excitement and started relaxing in place of the worry. What was important was that you were *trying* to get excited.

Do this exercise:

Imagine you're in a Ferrari on the open road, and you're going thirty miles an hour. Keep it at thirty and see what happens. Most people experience a relaxed feeling as they fail the potential excitement of the Ferrari. Some of you, however, downshifted and stuffed your foot to the floor and got excited, followed by Miller Time. This is an example of a good no-lose situation because when you think excitement, you either get excited and that feels good, or you get relaxed and that feels good too. That's why when you leave the land of worry and enter the land of excitement . . . you can't lose. One of two good things will happen.

With the Ferrari you were "trying" to get thirty miles an hour of excitement out of the car, and like all trying . . . it failed. But you want failure in this case because it makes you feel relaxed without effort. If you did this thirty-miles-an-hour fantasy in a Yugo, it wouldn't work. You need the element of potential excitement. As long as you are going in the adrenaline direction, you are not trying to control the ANS, and you get the results *you* want.

Now that you know this failed excitement loophole for relaxation, you can use it deliberately as a relaxation technique under pressure. Expect to fail and win!

When I first began charting my excitement on the biofeedback equipment, I used the fantasy of doing a wheelie on a motorcycle at speed. It gave me that thrilling feeling and I felt alive. It was great for getting rid of worries. Eventually, though, I got used to the thrill so I made it more risky. I put the bike on a hairpin turn in the Alps. In time that fantasy burned out too, so now I use it for relaxation!

Chapter 9

INSOMNIA MODEL

$\mathcal{T}$ his insomnia model makes use of the two positive misuses of the stress response (phantom excitement and failed excitement). The cause of insomnia
is the negative misuse of the stress response (phantom adrenaline) in a place (your bedroom) where
no real survival threat exists.

Classic psychological approaches to insomnia involve relaxation training, use of control factors,
which allow you to have control over the insomnia,
behavior retraining of presleep patterns, and strate-
gies for when you are awake in bed. Dealing with
insomnia's vicious cycle—the additional anxiety
created over the knowledge that you are unable to
sleep and will probably feel very tired come morn-

ing, which just adds to the insomnia—and the anger and resentment it creates is also important.

By using biofeedback, I can usually show clients their insomnia patterns while they are wide awake. I'll have them connected to galvanic skin response biofeedback that monitors the adrenaline in cold sweat gland activity. When relaxing a little, they will see and feel the adrenaline diminish and feel as though they could take a nap in a short time. Then I'll have them think of an upsetting thought. Instantly the BF meter will register phantom adrenaline, and the person will feel awake and alert. The adrenaline has an effect similar to a few cups of coffee. There is no nap in their immediate future now. This is what happens in bed when they worry, think upsetting thoughts, or start a vicious cycle about not sleeping.

It is at this point that relaxation would seem like a solution to their problem, since they felt okay and sleepy when they registered as relaxed. But that's hard to do. So they need to relax indirectly. Here's how:

> *The first thing I have them do is convert immediately to "good insomnia." Here's what*

I mean by good insomnia. Perhaps you can remember how you felt after a great first date with a special person. It may have even kept you up for a few nights thinking about him or her and how lucky you were. You couldn't sleep—but you didn't care! That's good insomnia.

When you're in bed with bad insomnia, all it takes is one exciting thought (risky or risqué) to instantly convert (relabel) to good insomnia. Now you have a smile on your face and you feel good, and are still awake, but don't care. Miller Time is just around the corner and will naturally follow and head you in the direction of sleep. If you sabotage yourself again with worry (phantom adrenaline), just take another swan dive into excitement and repeat the process, feeling the control you have over your feelings. Eventually Miller Time will get you to sleep. Meanwhile you are in control, so there is no need for the vicious cycle thinking.

The great part of this system is that if you can't get into the excitement, you get the failed excitement (relaxation) instead, which also takes you to sleep. You can't lose. You end up relaxed indirectly and have a system of staying in control of your autonomic nervous system. This way you'll either have a good night asleep or a good night awake!

Chapter 10

FEAR AND RISK— CHANGE AND THE RESISTANCE TO CHANGE

*W*hen we play it safe and don't risk anything, we don't have to deal with change and its threat to the security of the status quo. This false security may be okay, but it may also promote feelings of being stuck, bored, overwhelmed, unhappy, unfulfilled, resentful, angry, and fearful.

I would like you to take a look at fear and risk with me. To do that we must first fill out a list of positive exciting things you like to do or want to do. We will also list the good feelings you get when you do these exciting things.

Depending on the age group of those I ask, some examples of exciting things are hiking, skiing, traveling, learning, meeting new people, reaching new goals, sex, music, dancing, skydiving, driving fast, reading. This of course is just a partial list. Some of you would agree with some of the items, and not with others. If we write down the feelings associated with these exciting things we get a list that includes the following sensations: feeling alive, invigorated, challenged, fulfilled, stimulated, accomplished, connected, intimate, free, independent. What's interesting to note is that the activities change from person to person, but the good feelings list is always the same. If there is not enough of the good feelings list in your life, then read on. That list represents being alive in the world, not merely working, making money, resting, or feeling fear or anger about things you can't seem to change in yourself.

If you examine the exciting activities list you may notice that there is a risk or danger attached to doing those items. It may be hard to see at first because that risk may not be physical. It could be risking embarrassment being first out on the dance floor, or risking rejection when meeting someone new. The important point to remember is that when you do the exciting activity (risk the danger), you usually get the *entire* good feelings list!

Let's go skiing. Let's say I'm an average skier,

and I've never taken a little jump (catching air) before. I see a bunch of people having fun (excitement) skiing over a little mound of snow and landing. We're talking about a *really* little jump here, okay? If I want to get in on this fun, I must decide to take the risk and head toward the jump. How do I feel? The answer is scared, right? I feel anxious. "Am I going too fast?" "What if I crash?" "What if _____ ?" That's the voice of anxiety. I go into the future and create a disaster for my now body. Let's say that because of this anxiety, I chicken out at the last moment, taking a well-worn path that other scared first-timers made doing the same "bail out." What do I feel now? The answer is disappointment, shame, guilt, and mild depression. "I should have done it!" "If only I had taken the jump." Depression goes into the past and beats up the now body. So far, in attempting this little jump, I've experienced anxiety and depression. That's a wide range of emotional stress, and it's happening while I'm trying to have fun. What a bummer!

Now let's say through some miracle I make it through the anxiety and actually take the little jump. I successfully land. How do I feel? G-R-E-A-T! I got my good feelings list. "I caught some air! I am *so* cool!!!"

The jump I just took is the same as the skydive example in the phantom excitement chapter. When I was feeling anxiety while approaching the ski jump, I didn't want to feel it, it just happened. When I felt excited upon landing, I didn't say that I would, it just happened. I also didn't even wonder where the fear went when I landed. It was G-O-N-E.

> Now let's take that same jump again. Do I feel any different approaching the jump this time? Yes. I feel confident. "I can do this! This is going to be cool!" That's the voice of positive anticipation, not relaxation. I'm talking about the excitement I'm going to get. That's the very thing that was on my mind when I first saw people having fun on the jump. I've naturally relabeled the fear, anxiety, risk, and danger as phantom excitement. When I land I will feel great again!

Learning to control this relabeling is the purpose of this chapter. It allows us to take risks in life better. Many times we take a risk only once. We have to pay our dues by feeling anxious the first time (fear of unknown). What you should do is relabel the fear as the "price of admission" for the excitement you are about to have, because that's what it is. If you don't do something (any change in your life) you are feeling the anxiety and stopping before the jump. You are paralyzed by the fear. You just did the *hardest part* and left before the excitement! How many times do we do this to ourselves and *never* get the payoff? You have a right to get your good feelings list. The anxious feeling *is supposed to be there* the first time. Just see it for what it is, the price you pay for the excitement of the good feelings list you are about to get.

We are a society of prescription cures and bad-habit cures. To quell the anxiety of a first-time little ski jump you could take a Xanax or a Valium, but you'd be missing out on the excitement of the other side when you land! If you want the excitement of that landing *without* having to take the risk, you could just take an upper like cocaine. Using the ski jump model, we can see how it is misused with drugs. For instance, you want the excitement (cocaine) without taking the risk, which you would get naturally from the landing. Both these false solutions avoid or drug the "living" part of life by sedating that part of life or artificially pumping it. Life was given to you to enjoy naturally. By under-

CRAIG B. MARDUS, PH.D.

standing and applying this model, you can feel better about the challenge of life and *how* to live it.

> *Positive anticipation is the mark of an optimist. Negative anticipation is the cynic's view.*

If you take that ski jump fifty times you will notice that you begin to feel bored on the approach. This translates to feeling bored on the landing as well. Now it's time to find a bigger jump. As the risk goes away, so does the living (excitement).

Some real-life examples of taking emotional risks include the following: saying no, asking for help, expressing feelings, being more assertive, losing weight, curbing a bad habit, dealing with anger.

Let's flip a pen! A great way to demonstrate the difference between playing it safe, self-abuse, boredom, and anxiety on the one hand, and risk, excitement, and self-care on the other is to flip a pen. What?

Take an ordinary ballpoint pen that is ready to write. Gently give it a small flip in the air and catch it. Do it again. And again. Make it simple and easy to do, over and over. This represents playing it safe, no risk, on the verge of boredom. With time you can even do it with your eyes closed. This represents a life of no change and playing it safe. When I do this demonstration, I playact the following script while I casually flip the pen with a bored expression on my face: "I get up in the morning . . . feel tired. I go to work . . . work's a pain. I look at my watch . . . it's only 10:00 A.M.? I finally finish work . . . boy, am I exhausted! I go home . . . overeat at dinner . . . feel too full. God, I've got to lose weight one of these days! I have no energy . . . I'll watch TV . . . nothing's on. Time for bed . . . oh, no . . . insomnia again! I get up . . . feel real tired, etc. . . ."

That's the nonrisking (nonliving) script that a lot of people can relate to. Now, if I want to introduce risk to this pen flip, what do I have to do? That's right. I have to flip it way up there near the ceiling. At this point (risk), I have two choices that, depending on my initial choice, can also lead to two more choices. The first two choices after that B-I-G F-L-I-P are: 1) to catch the pen and feel alive ("I did it!"), or 2) to miss it. If I miss it, the two new choices are: 1) to beat myself up, or 2) to enjoy the journey toward catching it.

Let me play out what I might say to myself if I keep missing several big flips in a row and then catch it finally: "Boy, I stink at this! I can't believe

I missed that one. Ouch, that hurt! I'm such a klutz. I'm never going to get it. There, I finally got lucky . . . big deal." That is an example of being hard on yourself, putting yourself down. When you finally catch it, you don't even feel good!

> *The second option (to enjoy the journey) relies on the* fact *that you will eventually catch it (the destination), and it will be exciting once you do. This script is one of self-care, self-nurturance, and self-encouragement. "Almost got it then! Any second now! Nice try! I can do it! It's going to feel so cool when I get it! Yes! I got it!"*

Since, however, many risks involving a life change may not be transferred instantly to excitement, it is necessary to take that second option for your journey. It might take time to become more assertive, to stop smoking, to lose weight, to share your feelings, but it *will* be worth the journey!

> *Choose the journey, understand the need for risk, and feel great when you eventually arrive!*

Chapter 11

BURNING OUT AN ANXIETY

T his is another ANS trick you can use in addition to the Mardus Maneuver. It will work because you're not trying to get rid of anxiety directly, but rather indirectly by using the autonomic nervous system to help you instead of sabotage you (its main directive when you try to control it).

> Let's go to the drive-in. The moment you notice you are worrying about something, imagine you are at a drive-in movie theater. Decide to worry on purpose *for twenty seconds. Let them show the movie (visualization) of your worry on the big screen. Make it as bad as possible and feel the tension in your*

body. After the twenty seconds, let the drive-in show one of those refreshment commercials popular in the 1950s, you know, the ones showing all the talking hamburgers, hot dogs, and french fries telling you the show will start again soon, so hurry up and visit the refreshment stand! Watch this amusing short for twenty seconds and then go back to the main feature—your worry. Watch it for twenty seconds and feel the tension in your body. Alternate twenty seconds of the worry movie with twenty seconds of the refreshment short, and you will find that by the fourth or fifth interval you won't be able to worry as much. You will still see the worry movie, but your body has gotten tired of feeling bad. Your body lets your worry go.

This exercise works for temporary relief or burn-out of the anxiety mainly because it gives you *control* of the worry movie. You are deciding to run the movie at the drive-in. By doing this activity *on purpose*, you take most of the bad reflex of worry and hurt away from your body as a result of this element of control. The ANS "helps" you do this because it thinks you are going to get more and more worried—but it's wrong! You are using its response to burn the worry out. By taking that creative, funny refreshment break, you give yourself some busy time in between the worries, once again *not* trying to relax (which the ANS hates for you to do to its adrenaline). Keeping busy with an active, funny thought doesn't bother the ANS, it just puts it on hold for twenty seconds.

Both the Mardus Maneuver and the worry burnout work because they use adrenaline not relaxation to fix the problem.

Chapter 12

TWO TYPES OF CONTROL: UNDERSTANDING STRESS MANAGEMENT

*S*tress management is different from relaxation.

Relaxation helps you when you get tired from functioning (living fully) on a daily basis. It will not help you when you are in the midst of living in fear or anger. At best, it will act only as a temporary escape, much the same way drugs and depression do. Relaxation is preventive in the way it works (see relaxation chapter).

Stress management is what you do when you are *in* stress conflict. It is an attitude you develop about life's problems. It is an attitude of being assertive with life, not passive *or* aggressive with it. A good stress manager is a problem solver, is emotionally stable, has no addictions, sees life as a challenge, has a good self-image, has minimum aches and pains, and finds time to relax and play.

A poor stress manager dwells on problems, is either depressed or anxious, has one or more addictions, sees life through fear and anger, has a poor self-image, has several forms of chronic aches and pains, and is always rushing.

The shift in attitude necessary to changing from being a poor stress manager to a good stress manager involves a deep understanding of the two types of control: external and internal. Control is a need that can either be deprived or fulfilled. Good stress managers fulfill their control needs internally, while poor stress managers try to fulfill theirs externally—and inevitably fail.

Let's take a step back and see the big picture. I define stress as people and things not going your way. Even you could be one of those people not going your way, as in the case of trying but failing to lose weight or becoming more assertive. You get stressed because people (including you) and things (like traffic jams or slow lines) are not going your way (under your direct control). This is called an external control issue. You would be happy (stress-free) *if* these things would just go your way. A very critical and thus angry person would tend to say,

"I'm really a very calm, nice person, if just everything would go my way" (be correct, on time, efficient).

But the reality is that people and things not going your way represents the flow of life. These things are not there to hurt you directly. They are just the flow of life that happens to push your stress button. I like to use the metaphor of the sun to explain this further. The sun is a good example of a daily life event. The one thing you're not supposed to do with the sun is to stare at it directly. If you do so it will hurt you. Staring or dwelling on life's problems will also hurt you in the form of stress-related symptoms. A stress dweller becomes a complainer, blamer, moaner, groaner, and whiner. The stress symptoms over time turn into chronic stress-related illnesses. Most causes of death are stress-related.

Just as you could put on sunglasses when the sun is too bright, you can do a lot to solve the problems of life from your point of view (internal control). This shift to internal control is what action, thoughts or feelings you can have that might start solving the stress problem. That action might even be to avoid the stress problem or do nothing about it! You have a lot of power if you use it instead of feeling overwhelmed by the aspects of life that are going to happen anyway, whether you are there or not (it's usually not personal in its intent).

Most life events that stress us (disappointment, a canceled meeting, delay, someone changing their mind, someone being late, making a mistake) are literally in the past the moment they happen. When we focus on external control, we are dwelling on the hurt and are really saying, "I'll only be happy now *if* the bad event disappeared." That will only happen in a cartoon—maybe!

A good stress manager voices the hurt, then solves the problem to the best of his or her internal control ability: "Darn. The plane's delayed an hour! (deep breath). I guess I'll make a few calls and pick up some magazines to read." Stress is now controlled. Note though, you are not supposed to feel relaxed when you use stress management, just a little more in control. This is important to understand. Whatever you do, think, or feel to make you more in control *after* the stress event, that's fully using your internal control. Now you're a stress manager.

It is important to voice your feelings the moment stress occurs and then take a deep breath. Let's face it, you're a little—or a lot—upset and need to honor that feeling. If you practice Zen, you might not feel upset, but just a shift in cosmic energy. You might even say that it is good that this stressful event happened for it was meant to be, and just another part of life. That's fine *if* you can do that, but most Americans get upset and want to do something about it. It is still necessary to honor the feelings and express them to yourself or out loud. "Boy, I'm pissed!" Then take a deep breath and shift to internal control and decide your best way to handle the problem.

Choosing to feel upset and express that feeling gives you power compared to the typical knee-jerk reaction of anger to these types of life events. When you plan and decide to always say you're upset, then breathe, you are starting the process of internal control. It's like that old *Saturday Night Live* bit with the two janitors who keep describing horrible things they would do to their bodies with drills, hammers, and screwdrivers, and then say, "I hate when that happens! It hurts like the dickens!" They did it, what else would they expect but it to hurt?

If you're in your thirties or older, I would chance it to say that your life problems are in "reruns" by now. It might be appropriate to just say, "This again?" Everything that happens on a daily level has probably happened before. Right? I'm talking about daily annoyances, not the death of a loved one. It's just a rerun. Don't react to it as though it were the first time. It probably isn't.

So just choose to say, "I hate when this happens," smile, and breathe (thinking about those *SNL* guys), and use your internal control to be a problem solver instead of an out-of-control problem dweller.

Chapter 13

TWO ROCK MODEL OF STRESS MANAGEMENT

$\mathcal{W}$hen we talked about using excitement to stop worrying in one second without effort, you were giving yourself a power you always had but never used. That ANS trick works when you are alone worrying (in a perfectly good now).

My Two Rock Model of stress management is what I use when I am in conflict, stress, or control battles with another person in the now. The Two Rock Model is a further modification of the problem solver model of the two types of control theory.

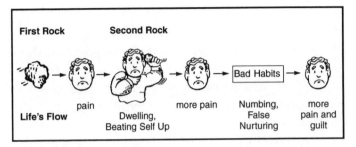

The stress model outlined above shows life throwing you a rock (stress). It is out of your control. It hurts, but now it is a nanosecond in the past and can't be changed (reversed). You then pick up this rock (we'll call this the second rock) and beat yourself with it (dwell, complain, moan, groan, put yourself down), causing M-O-R-E P-A-I-N! The pain is so great now (anxiety, depression, frustration, disappointment) that you usually will grab for a bad habit to make you feel better in a false way. You might reach for food, drugs, alcohol, cigarettes, sleep, anger, depression, anxiety, or too much of anything (work, exercise) to give yourself the illusion that you are helping yourself and in control. These bad habits all hurt the body. They act as numbing agents for the immediate pain, but cause even more pain and guilt afterward. That is the stress cycle people are in who say they have a lot of stress in their life. They are trying (failing) to cure it with a bad coping skill (habit). It helps them cope temporarily but at the expense of their body. Good coping skills help you cope and feel in control as you do what you can to help care for your body in a functional way. Going with the flow of life from your control point is the functional way to avoid pain and guilt. That's what we really want. It involves challenges and risks that we must be willing to take.

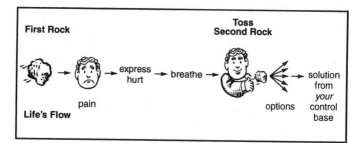

The stress manager model goes like this: The same rock is thrown at you by life. No one can change that. It hurts. It's supposed to. You self-express the hurt ("I hate when this happens"), realize it is probably a rerun ("this again?"), and pick up the rock (second rock now) and begin to toss it in the air repeatedly.

This tossing represents you deciding what you want to do with it (the problem that is now in the past). You go over your options of dealing with it, handling it, coping with it, solving it. The two things you must not do are: 1) throw it away and tell yourself it never happened (denial), or 2) jump in a hot tub (the rock/ problem needs your attention now).

Reviewing and deciding which options to use accesses your personal internal control, and you feel a little good adrenaline when you are doing, thinking, and feeling on your own terms. That's all you get or are supposed to get using stress management. You are not supposed to feel relaxed or that you can reverse the flow of the world. That is what seriously stressed-out people think and believe—which is why they experience such stress. When you engage in solving the problem, you begin to feel some control over something over which you thought you had no control.

Your options are specific to your assertive powers of behavior. Let's go over these powers in detail and also look at why some of us feel we can't use them. These failures to *not* use your options are the "Myths of Dysfunction." We learned them in childhood and now they are our beliefs. These dysfunctional beliefs are based on passive or aggressive behavior instead of assertive behavior.

Assertive Versus Dysfunctional Behavior

Options (Tossing the Rock) Assertive Powers of Behavior	Myths of Dysfunction (Passive or Aggressive Behavior)
1. I can say no. That will give the problem back to someone else. It's okay to sometimes say no.	1. I can't say no. People won't like me. I won't be a nice person. I have to help everyone and put myself last.
2. I can ask for help to solve this problem. Sometimes we need help and it's okay to ask.	2. I'll look weak if I ask for help. I can do it all myself and be the strong person I need to be at all times.
3. I can take a break and come back to this problem. I'll return with	3. I can't take time out for breaks. That's for lazy people who run

a fresh outlook and see solutions easier.	away from problems. That's not me.
4. I can express my feelings, anger, or annoyance. The world needs to know how I'm feeling about what just happened.	4. I have to keep my feelings to myself. That way I'm in control. No one will ever know I'm upset.
5. I can ask questions for clarification. If I know more about what's going on, I'll see a solution faster.	5. If I ask a lot of silly questions, I'll look stupid and incompetent. I'm better off shutting up.
6. I can delegate some or all of this problem to someone else. Chances are they will do at least an adequate job. If not, I can still handle it.	6. If I delegate it, the job won't be done right. No one can do it as well as I can. I'll just work harder and do it all myself.
7. I can wait a little and get more information on this problem before I invest in getting upset. It might be nothing.	7. I should know everything there is to know now. What good is more information going to do me? *continued*

8. I can use humor to help offset the tension of the moment.	8. There's no place for humor when I'm feeling stressed. This is really serious stuff, and I have to act like a grown-up.
9. I can reframe this as a challenge or opportunity. If I take the long view, this problem may prove to be a growth experience for me. It's a lesson in disguise.	9. There's only a short view and it's full of stress. There's only one way of looking at this. It's a crisis!
10. I can imagine how another person might handle this better than I can. I'll find a creative solution.	10. There's only one way to see this, and it's not good. I should know how to fix this myself.
11. I can reassure myself that this is just one of life's hassles, and that my self-esteem and identity can't be touched by this event. It can only be strengthened.	11. My identity right now is that of a failure. I won't be okay until this is behind me. This is wrong and I am wrong. I hate when things don't go my way.

continued

12. I can allow this problem to happen, exist, and end without any action on my part. Admitting that I can do nothing to change it allows me to accept it as part of the flow of life.	12. Now I really feel stuck! I can't do anything, and I feel like a victim. I'm never supposed to feel powerless.

The Two Rock Model tells you that you have no control over the first rock, but much control over the second. How you choose to use that second rock will either solve your problem or make you a victim of the first rock.

Chapter 14

THE THREE ELEMENTS OF LIFE

$\mathcal{J}$ see life as containing three elements: living, dying, and resting. "Living" I define as functioning psychologically, emotionally, spiritually in a positive way. Functional work, relationships, play, fun, chores, difficult times—all represent getting through life with a positive management of stress attitude. It is being assertive of all your personal rights and skills.

"Dying" I define as dysfunctioning in those same areas by being passive or aggressive in your approach to life. That will bring on a chronic condition of almost every negative emotion you can imagine. It also brings many forms of addiction to help numb all the pain and guilt.

"Resting" I define as relaxation—actively or passively letting the body and mind recuperate and regroup because they are tired.

How these three relate to each other is important. I see life (on a good day) as doing (functioning) a lot, getting tired, resting, feeling renewed, and going back to some more positive activity. This could be translated as getting up, having a good breakfast, going to work, communicating well, accomplishing what you want to, dealing with problems from your internal control, expressing your feelings if stress attacks, connecting with yourself and others, challenging yourself with new goals and risks, being tired at the end of the day, resting in some way (time out, reading, exercise, meditation, warm bath, music), feeling renewed, having an evening meal, bonding with family, discussing problems and solutions, doing some play activity, feeling tired again, going to bed. That would be an ideal day of functioning, resting, and functioning.

I see life (on a really bad day) as dying a lot: waking up tired, resting the wrong way, and feeling burnout and despair. For example: getting up with resentment and anger, skipping breakfast, going to work with a bad attitude, eating sugary or fatty snacks for relaxation, overworking your body, taking and giving abuse, going home and overeating at dinner, feeling lethargic, avoiding family in search of peace, getting into arguments, feeling exhausted, crashing to sleep and then insomnia. That's the worst scenario.

Even proper relaxation cannot recapture that day.

> *Only by switching from dysfunction to function, from dying to living, can you find the answer. Then you'll only get tired instead of burnt-out. Let your motto be: "LIVE, REST, LIVE."*

Chapter 15

BREATHING MODEL

$\mathcal{I}$ must admit that I didn't place much emphasis on breathing as a relaxation technique when I first learned about it. I was greatly surprised in a session years ago when a high-powered entrepreneur sat in the leather reclining chair, put his feet up on the windowsill, and commenced to tell me how much stress he was under. He told me not to waste his valuable time with gimmicks such as biofeedback, hypnosis, visualization, or relaxation techniques. He had tried them all with no success. He also mentioned he was in long-term therapy with one of the greats that I had studied in grad school. I had forty-nine minutes left in a fifty-minute session and no cards left up my sleeve. He was in obvious denial as to helping himself, so stress management was going to seem too challenging. He was looking for a magic cure of the external variety.

With a stutter in my voice, I suggested diaphragmatic breathing. He told me to tell him more about it. Not only did it work well to relax him, he loved it as well. It opened the door in follow-up sessions to some good work in biofeedback and visualization. He couldn't wait to get back home to tell his therapist about breathing. From that point on I became a believer in diaphragmatic breathing.

If a person arrives at a session in tears or in deep emotional reaction, we just sit and breathe together for a few minutes first. It gives them the relaxation and control to start telling their story.

I have, in fact, developed my own particular view of breathing as a technique that can be learned easily. I learned a lot from smokers, kids, close calls, swimmers, and innocent murder defendants in order to come up with this model. I guess this might require a little explaining:

I see breathing as having three parts: the inhale, the exhale, and the glide. When you are relaxed you are unaware that you are even breathing. Your breathing is being controlled for you by our friend the autonomic nervous system. The glide part, the tail end of the exhale that gets longer the more relaxed you are, is so smooth when you are relaxed that you hardly notice the transition from exhale to inhale. You don't notice the need to breathe when you are relaxed or lost in an activity. Swimmers know this feeling when they relax underwater.

When you start to feel uneasy (stress throws you a rock) the glide is the first thing to disappear, quickly followed by the exhale. You are left inhaling and inhaling. You are actually holding your breath just as you did as a kid when you were upset. You'd be turning red, complaining about what went wrong at school or what your brother borrowed and won't return. Parents know this look in kids very well. As an adult perhaps you dove into a cold pool, and when you surfaced you might have said (with a high, held breath), "Boy, it's cold in here!" If only you had exhaled then, the water would have seemed much warmer. As an adult you probably don't realize that you still hold your breath when upset.

If I were to sneak up on you and scare you by surprise (close call), I would bet that you would gasp an inhale that was audible. Try to imagine yourself exhaling during that moment and you'll find it to be impossible. So we know that stress comes in on an inhale. We keep inhaling until we are holding our breath and don't know it. All we know is that we are having trouble breathing. We either remain in this state of anxiety or go into "manual override" and correct the problem.

If you watch an innocent murder defendant in court when the jury is giving their decision, you'll notice two things: When the jury foreman says, "The verdict is . . ." the defendant starts an inhale and holds his breath. When the foreman says "not guilty," the person exhales a sigh of deep relief and starts to feel better immediately. That's how powerful breathing can be. That is what we need to do in manual override breathing. Exhale first and then start diaphragmatic breathing on purpose (using the central nervous system, CNS).

The inhale is not always supposed to feel good. Life has conditioned you repeatedly that stress equals inhale. It is designed to save your life by giving you oxygen. You can make your breathing more comfortable if you push your belly out when inhaling instead of raising your shoulders as during a nervous upper-body inhale. This belly inhale allows the diaphragm to move away from the solar plexus nerve complex in your stomach area and thus take the pressure off. This inhale is designed to take in air and relieve pressure. An inhale may still seem somewhat stressful because of its lifelong connection with close-call gasps. The exhale however has a lifelong connection with relief. Just say "not guilty" to yourself and feel the effect in the exhale. Exhales feel great! We don't know how to give ourselves this gift during stress, but rather wait for some external sign of relief to start the exhale. Just do it deliberately and give yourself some relief now. You can override the automatic ANS breathing and breath holding with good old manual breathing.

Diaphragmatic breathing takes the hurt out of pain, either physical or emotional. That's why it is used in childbirth and anxiety attacks. If someone is hurt, get him or her breathing. Eventually the control goes back to the ANS and all is well and off alert status.

When a smoker takes a long, deep inhale from a cigarette, within seven seconds the nicotine, when administered with a diaphragmatic breath, causes the brain to release serotonin and dopamine, which makes the person feel relaxed. Nicotine is unique as a drug because it can act as either a stimulant or relaxant de-

pending on how it is administered. That has to do with breathing style. Smokers already know how to diaphragmatically breathe if they are using the cigarettes for relaxation. If you just took a deep diaphragmatic breath of air you would also get some serotonin and dopamine in seven seconds. The nicotine acts as a turbocharger for the reaction. My theory learned from smokers is that as they get anxious they unknowingly start holding their breath. They reach for a cigarette to give themselves a structured way to start breathing. That's why that first exhale feels so good to them. All you need is an awareness that a structured breathing system is needed when you are getting upset. That way you can use the power of breathing to start reversing the tension caused by holding your breath.

When I was a medic in the armed services, I would see guys hold their breath and tense up just before I gave them a shot. They were actually just creating more anxiety and making the shot more painful. Exhale first and the shot hurts less. The times they were in conversation with one of the nurses, they barely noticed the shot.

Chapter 16

FLOATING AS A PRIME RELAXER

$\mathcal{M}$an has always wanted to fly. There is a good reason for that. Have you ever had a great dream where you realized that you could float or fly and were having a wonderful time? That dream's a keeper! Subconsciously during the dream, your mind might have said, "This is impossible, I can't fly!" But your body was saying, "Don't worry. It's okay. Enjoy the light, free feeling. I am."

It's easy for your body to say this because it is based on past experience. It's been there before. Let me explain. We all floated for nine months before birth in the safest, most secure, nurturing, need-fulfilling environment of all time—the womb. That is the body memory that is going on when we have that dream or enjoy any floating experience: a boat ride, relaxing on a float in a pool, on a rocking chair, skiing, hang gliding . . . the list goes on.

Most clichés and words that indicate lift and lightness are positive psychologically: walking on air, head in the clouds, up, high, free, weightless, uplifting, elevated. Most negative psychological issues are in the other direction: down, stuck, heavy, depressed, grounded, dragging, sinking, falling, downtrodden, overladen.

Narcotics also give you a sense of the floating feeling. They are known for their I-don't-care-about-the-pain ability. You are lifted above the hurt and the pain. Endorphins released in exercise do the same when maximized (see next chapter).

With experiences of deep relaxation, one is made aware that the body is getting heavy and warm while the person (spirit) feels light and buoyant.

To maximize this ANS floating gift we sometimes get, I suggest you practice imaging your favorite floating scenario as a way to find deep peace in our natural desire to return to the security of the womb. I always use images of floating in hypnosis because I believe they are the most powerful trance state for relax-

ation. The ANS body memory is working for you unconsciously. And any real activity that involves floating can have increased value for you once you know this state allows you to feel at ease. So find your special floating or flying image and notice the natural floating sensation following an uplifting experience.

Chapter 17

MAXIMIZING EXERCISE: MISSING ANS LINKS

$\mathcal{I}$f you asked a large group of people about their attitudes and feelings concerning aerobic exercise, you would be surprised at the variety of responses you would get. Some hate it. Some love it. Some are bored, while others are focused. Some procrastinate over it, while others encourage themselves to do it. Some feel just okay afterward, while others feel energized or deeply relaxed.

There seemed to me to be too much variance for just one type of activity, so I asked some more questions, did some research, and discovered some common ground to explain all this to my satisfaction.

When we were kids, we used to run, jump, get sweaty, energized, and relaxed. We called this "play." When school started we had gym class where we did some exercises and something called the President's Fitness Program. Now our play was getting too structured and involved. It was full of fierce competition, nervousness, losing, failing, and worrying about succeeding and passing; it felt a lot like "work." Later we found exercise used as a form of punishment if late for class or when in the army (push-ups or running laps). As adults we return to the world of exercise with many mixed emotions as to what it really is. Add to that the built-in boredom of most aerobic equipment, and we lose that original feeling of play we had as kids.

In many cases, I found that those who hated exercise had gotten gypped out of their share of play as a child. Either they lived in a high rise in the city or had overprotective parents, had too much responsibility placed on them at too early an age, or had too much fear in their lives as a result of abuse or trauma. Any of those could contribute to feeling a loss of the joy of being a kid and playing. That feeling can be newly experienced by allowing yourself fun in exercise.

It's never too late to have a happy childhood.
Start off by taking a pool aerobics class, box-

ercise, or dancercise, and see if the music, group bonding, and fun instill that sense of lost play. If you use one of those aerobic pieces of equipment, add music, adventure books on tape, TV, phone conversations, or fantasies to the workout. For me, the built-in digital displays just aren't enough to avoid the inevitable boredom from a repetitive task. So the first step is to instill, find, or rediscover the play part of exercise. The body really loves to move. Ask any dancer or person in the audience of a rock concert or musical.

Aerobic exercise is a form of active relaxation. Since it *is* a form of relaxation, you are never too tired to exercise. You are never too tired to relax! (See the procrastination chapter to discover a simple way to get to the gym.)

When you do aerobic exercise, which means you reach and stay at a target heart rate while moving the long muscles of the body (legs and arms), while doing correct breathing, you get three things: cardiovascular fitness, weight loss (from fat), and release of endorphins.

Endorphins are neurotransmitters released in the brain from aerobic exercise or laughter. They are not usually realized during nonaerobic or stop-and-go sports (tennis, golf). Endorphins use the same receptor sites as most morphine-based narcotics. They are for all purposes a natural narcotic. That is why aerobic instructors are so cheery.

I have a piece of electromedical equipment, which is called a CES, or Cranial Electrical Stimulation, machine, that was designed for chronic-pain control. It uses the principle of cranial electrical stimulation to release your own endorphins so that you don't "care" as much about your pain. That "I don't care" attitude is how narcotics work. (The typical patient's response to morphine is: "The pain's still there, but I don't care!")

I noticed that when I was working with patients using the CES machine that they were having difficulty paying attention to me when they had this device on. They really just wanted me to shut up so they could take a nap! That was the endorphins talking.

Applying this information to aerobic exercise, you will notice that you may feel the same way after just twenty minutes of aerobics. For many people, that's the magic number for the ANS to release your endorphins. Any more workout would be for cardiovascular fitness or weight loss. Any less and the endorphins won't be released. To get the deeply relaxed effect of the endorphins, all you need is twenty minutes.

When you ask people what they do *after* their aerobic workout, they will usually mention one of the following: stretch, drink water, talk to someone, shower, sauna, drive their car on errands, or return home or to work. The endorphins put you into an alpha brain wave state where you really don't want to attend to anything very important. I noticed the same effect with the CES machine.

> *To honor your body and get the most out of the relaxation aspect of aerobics, you need to do the following* directly *after your workout (twenty minutes or more): find a place to lie down; close your eyes; listen to music or nothing; and enjoy the floating narcotic effect of the endorphins you just released. This way you stay in an alpha state and get an almost meditative effect. It seems to last for twenty minutes or so. You will be too relaxed to even sleep during that time. After that you can sleep a wonderful sleep, or shower, stretch, work out with weights, whatever. That will put you back into a beta brain wave state where you*

> *want to* attend *to people and things. You leave*
> *the "I don't care" state.*

Anxiety and depression can't live in an alpha state. It feels good. This is a very important trick of the ANS. You will also get a residual effect of the endorphin release for up to twenty-four hours. That is why you feel better on a day that you work out. But if you do that twenty minutes of endorphin appreciation *after* that workout, you will maximize the total effect or high of the endorphins. The workout is like doing the work. The twenty minutes of endorphin appreciation is like getting your paycheck, and the twenty-four hours of residual time-released endorphins are like small dividends. Don't leave work without your paycheck!

When you alter your after-workout routine this way, you will have a whole new attitude about aerobic exercise.

The next question is when to do your aerobic/ endorphin workout. To answer this I'd like to describe the usual day of highly stressed people: They get up feeling rested or sluggish. They go to work, deal with stress correctly or not, and by 6:00 P.M. they get the attitude or feeling that all their work energy has been used up. They'll say, "If that phone rings one more time," or, "If someone wants one more thing from me . . . I'll just scream!" "I just want to go home and RELAX!" That is what I call the "all-demanded-out syndrome." When that person does go home, they find out that relaxation is *not* waiting for them as they had hoped. Rather, it is their *second job* that is waiting for them! They now have a few hours of new demands (mail, phone messages, family, problems, paperwork, bills, leaky faucets, and an assortment of life's broken shoelaces) placed on their already demanded-out system. They usually use dinner as a source of reward and relaxation and thus overeat. Then they might feel lethargic, waste time napping or watching TV, and crash to bed exhausted, only to find insomnia. That is the worst scenario.

What their body really needed when it was all demanded-out was rest and relaxation. That is the perfect time for exercise/endorphins. You get deep rest, feel renewed, and are able to take on the demands of your "second job." Doing the exercise "between jobs" is when you need it most. That way you will avoid needing the heavy meal as your false relaxation and will have energy at night and sleep more restfully.

Another incentive for doing exercise in the late afternoon or early evening is that circadian rhythms (daily mind/body cycles) tell us that the body is most pain-tolerant and strong in the late afternoon. If you ever get captured by the enemy and are going to be tortured . . . ask for the 5:00 P.M. slot! Since exercise/endorphins is a system of relaxation, we really don't want to do it early in the morning or late at night since we either just got sleep or are about to get it. Sleep is our main daily source of relaxation, but, because of dream activity in sleep, about an hour is missing each day. That is why we need that extra hour. It is in the middle of your waking day that you could really use that extra hour and that connects with the late afternoon as well.

Daily aerobic exercise was designed to be part of our lifestyle naturally. Whether it was churning butter, chopping wood, or walking fast to school or work, we used to get our daily requirement. Our civilized age has made these obsolete for most of us, so we have to schedule special time to get aerobic. In the movie *L.A. Story*, Steve Martin walks to his car, gets in, drives twenty feet, parks, gets out, and walks to his neighbor's door! How's that for progress?

Exercise/endorphins is a natural antidepressant and anti-anxiety treatment. How many aerobic instructors do you know who are on Prozac or Xanax? It's a nice way of using your ANS with your CNS.

Chapter 18

PROCRASTINATION MODEL

$\mathcal{W}$ hether it's exercise, getting up in the morning, cleaning the house, paying your bills, or changing a light bulb, it can be intolerable when you add the self-inflicted anxiety of procrastination. The logic works this way: "I just don't seem to be able to get to do it." "There are a whole bunch of reasons why I can't, now." "It seems overwhelming." "I know I'll feel better when it's done, but that doesn't seem to help me now." "I don't have the energy, time, resources to get it done now." All these are the voice of procrastination. It's a script of anxiety, negative anticipation, and depression—our old friends (normal nuts).

*To understand and short-circuit this re-
sponse, it is important to see the two stages
that exist with everything we do. First, there's
the thinking about doing stage (anticipation,
positive or negative). Then there's the actual
doing stage. The doing stage can take from one
second to years.*

Most or all the anxiety lives in the first stage, the
thinking stage. That's how we define anticipation:
emotional investment in the future (positive or negative). All the excuses, denial, rationalizations live
in the thinking about doing stage. They can't exist
in the second (doing) stage.

For example, if you are in bed, and the alarm
goes off, and you hit the snooze button a couple
of hundred times, you are the kind of person we
would call a procrastinator about getting up in the
morning. In that bed you'll feel some anxiety/de-
pression, hear a bunch of really great excuses, and
almost convince yourself that you can stay there
indefinitely! The moment you actually get up and
stand by the side of your bed, however, it is no
longer an issue. It's done. You're up. No more
anxiety about getting up exists now because you
have entered the doing stage and did it.

Now you might be procrastinating about having to take a shower. Once you're in the shower, again, it's no longer a problem because you are doing it. You're in the doing stage.

It's really easy to see how this works for quickly accomplished activities, but it also works for more time-consuming tasks or projects. For example, say I'm procrastinating about cleaning up my house; if I just walk over and pick up my jeans and put them in the hamper, I am doing and feeling a lot better already.

> *Doing (taking action) is like living (functioning). Thinking about doing (anticipation anxiety) is like dying (dysfunctioning) in the Two Rock Stress Model discussed previously. You make the switch from dysfunction to function and it feels good. Now you're living instead of worrying about living. The added bonus is the very good (almost great) feeling you get when the task or project is done.*

An enhanced modification of this technique is to make an automatic choice to go directly into the doing stage for five minutes, then decide if you want to continue doing it or not. That way you are deciding (thinking) in the doing stage where there is much less or no anxiety. To use this modification in the exercise example, it would work like this:

> *You make an automatic choice (this means you just do it!) to go to the gym after work four specific days a week, put on your sneakers and workout clothes, and get your butt on that machine for five minutes. Then, you ask yourself (if you remember to) if you want to work out or not. Most times you will say yes. All the excuses melt away because you are lost (absorbed) in the doing (living) stage. If you usually use the excuse that you don't have enough energy to work out, you will discover that your needed energy is waiting for you five minutes into the doing stage! Give that a chance to happen, then make your decision. Some of you have done this technique by mistake and discovered the power of just doing it. Nike was right!*

In all procrastination, just take a jump into the doing stage without using your brain and turn it on five minutes later. Things will look a whole lot better.

Chapter 19

ANGER TRAINING

$\mathcal{I}$f you ask a large group of people in an audience attending a talk on "dealing with anger" how they express their anger, you will usually come up with two types of responses: internalizing (keeping it in) or yelling (getting it out). Rarely will you get the functional answer, which we'll come to shortly.

It's important to understand the dynamics of what's happening when we feel angry and what happens when we choose a particular way of expressing it. It's a pretty complicated subject that I have given special study, so please be patient as I tell the story. It really needs to be told.

I believe that all anger is valid, and that expressing it functionally keeps it valid. When we express it dysfunctionally we either hurt ourselves or others. There are internalizers (we'll call them stuffers) and externalizers (we'll call them yellers). It's easy to be a combination of these two as well. You could stuff for a long time, then yell (long-fuse person). You can stuff with acquaintances and yell at family or vice versa. You could stuff with authority figures and yell at peers and subordinates, or any other combo platter you might imagine.

Anger is the main stress emotion. It's important to understand its dynamics. If I ask that audience, "Who keeps their anger in?" I'll usually get silence while they are thinking about whether or not it's the "right" answer. Then I'll make it easier for them to answer by adding, "Those of you who keep it in are probably in control, and no one's going to see you lose control or even know you are upset." Now I'll get some hands as they proudly display their "control." They think, "Yeah, I'm doing it right!"

Then I'll ask the same audience, "Who lets their anger out and yells?" Silence again as they size up whether it's the right answer or not. Then I sweeten the pot again and add, "Those of you who yell know that's the best way. Get it out so you won't get an ulcer or heart attack. That's what doctors will tell you." Now the hands come up quickly. "Yeah, we get it out!"

I ask for any other choices, and sometimes I'll get the answer I'm seeking: "I usually let the person know I'm angry, and tell them what it was that made me angry." Self-expression of the feeling and relating it to what just happened. For example: "You know, I'm a little upset now. I really didn't like it when you overlooked me when it was time to make that decision." Or: "I'm angry over your taking the car without asking." Or: "It really hurts me when you forget my birthday." This is the assertive expresser of anger.

Let's take a look at what we want to accomplish, consciously or unconsciously, when we are angry. There's a four-part list: 1) You want your body to feel better (more in control). 2) You want to bring the source of the anger closer to you. 3) You want to get some form of apology, understanding, explanation, or communication from the other person. 4) You want to avoid any guilt. Let's first examine what the stuffer and yeller do and how they miss out achieving the goals on the list.

Stuffers are specialists in self-abuse. They are passive in their expression of anger and try to deny it. It's too risky for them to say they are angry. They withdraw and use the silent treatment. They tend to hold grudges, feel unappreciated, and punish themselves with their anger. They think that by not expressing their anger they avoid confrontation and loss of approval. The anger lingers like an acid.

Let's look at their list. 1) Their body doesn't feel better, just more angry. 2) They push away the source of anger by withdrawing emotionally. 3) There is no communication or apology from that pushed-away person. 4) They feel guilt about not confronting the other person or expressing their anger.

Yellers are specialists in abusing others and thus indirectly abusing themselves. They project their anger onto people and things. Yellers are usually highly critical and judgmental people living in an imperfect world. Their yelling style is one of blaming, scolding, demeaning, and aggression. They have an angry-parent sound. By yelling they think they are in control, but to all around them they are simply demonstrating being out of control.

Let's look at their list: 1) They think their body feels better, but they really hate losing control. 2) They push people away with abuse. 3) No one can apologize to or communicate with them because they are in fear or hatred at that moment. 4) They feel guilt afterward when they cool down. They then are overly nice (and a major source of FTD floral arrangements!) for a while after yelling. They don't tend to hold grudges, but make it easy for others to.

To understand how the assertive anger expresser achieves the four goals on the list, let's try a little experiment. Suppose you had a wonderful sister, and you really loved her a lot. Let's say she's seated next to you, and you're having a normal conversation with her. All of a sudden you notice a little tear in her eye. How do you feel? Do you want to get closer to her or further away? Do you want to help her or hurt her? If you answered that you wanted to get closer and help her, that was the functional answer.

Let's take a closer look at what happened. You wanted to get closer and help when you saw the tear. You felt concerned and wanted to know what the tear was about. What is a tear? A tear is a nonverbal self-expression of hurt. When we are angry we are hurting. The stuffer takes that hurt message and puts it on a dagger and stabs himself with it. The yeller takes that hurt message, puts it on a spear, and throws it at someone. A functional person catching that spear in the shoulder would read the message on it and say, "I see by this message that you are hurting from anger right now, but I really don't like the way you deliver your messages (the spear)."

If we translate the purity of the tear into a verbal message it would sound like this: "I'm upset now," or, "I'm hurting," or, "Boy, I'm angry!" or, "I'm feeling annoyed." When you add to that self-expression—the tear—an explanation of what the cause was (the event or deed), then the source of your anger (the other person) knows how you feel *and* why you're feeling that way. Most of the time (if the other person cares about you) the other person will do the same thing you did with your sister: want to get closer and help. This is why anger training works.

Let's check the list to see what happens when you assertively self-express your anger and relate it to what just happened (the deed): 1) Your body feels better (more in control) by getting the anger out functionally (by talking for yourself). 2) You bring the source of anger closer (wanting to help or understand your hurt). 3) There is communication, problem solving, explanation, or apology available during this closeness (wanting to help). 4) There doesn't need to be any guilt because you've done what you need to do to express your feelings.

This little tear experiment can be used in a practical way as well. Some of my sessions are with young mothers and the anger they have with their little kids who are driving them crazy, to the brink of making yellers out of them. I explain that their yelling is only making enemies of their kids and to try this strategy:

> *The next time the kids are being too loud, messy, unorganized, hyper, and so forth, just let them see you go to a nearby corner and pretend to cry a little. I guarantee that within a minute or two there will be a tug at your jeans with a small person asking what's wrong. The nonverbal expression of your hurt allows them to help you. Now you can say, "You know, all that noise (activity, mess) really makes me upset. What can we do about it?"*
>
> *When those kids are making noise, being hyper, or being messy, one thing's for sure: they're not doing it exclusively to get you angry!*
>
> *Please read that sentence over again. We*

tend to react to it as though it were done sadisti-
cally to us. People are just "living their lives"
and inadvertently pushing your available but-
tons (the restrictions you place on your own
happiness).

If I am tapping my teeth with my pen while I'm trying to remember something to tell you, and that tapping is driving you crazy, one thing's for sure, and that is that I'm not tapping to get you upset. I'm tapping to help me think better. It's a habit, not a form of torturing you! If you tell me (self-express) that it annoys you, then to the extent that I care about you (like loving your sister), I'll change my behavior for you.

I've asked many people if they believe anger can be turned off like a switch, instantly. Almost all say no, that it takes time to go away. I'd like to show you a situation that proves it *can* be switched off instantly.

> *Let's say you were calling someone on the*
> *phone, and they put you on hold. Most people*
> *would get annoyed and angry after a couple of*
> *minutes. If you don't, it's because you probably*

94

use a speaker phone and do some work or play while you are waiting. If you do get upset, it's probably because you are saying to yourself, "Why is this taking so long? This person's really rude. I wouldn't keep them waiting this long. They're doing this just to bug me!" You create a cloud of anger over your head in just a few minutes.

If that person who put you on hold got back on the phone and said, "Sorry to keep you waiting so long, but I had a call on my other line that my sister was in a car accident, and I wanted to find out the details. What can I do for you?"

What do you think would happen to your anger? It would get turned to dust. It's off like a switch. It's probably now replaced with a "feeling stupid" feeling over the fact that you invested so much emotion and anger in the situation to begin with. All you needed was an apology and an explanation and your anger went away. When you express your anger and what it's about in the self-expressive anger-training way, you get just that! Anger is gone and you're living again.

This example is to show you that it is possible to extinguish anger instantly. Most cases won't work that fast, but at least when you use anger training you're in the right frame of mind.

Basically, someone is living his life (being incompetent, slow, noisy, rude, hyper, controlling, late) and you decide you don't like it and get angry. That person usually isn't doing it to you, he's just being himself. What's really happening is that your button (expectation of others) is being pushed *by you*. All that is needed is for you to share your button with that person, and to the extent they care about you, or want to change, they will talk to you about what they just did or said. It will usually come out quickly that it wasn't done to bug you.

The biggest fear a stuffer has is that when he takes the risk (going from passive to assertive) to say how he feels ("I feel upset over this") the other person will say one of the following: "Who cares!" "So what?" "You're oversensitive." "Get some therapy!" "That's your problem." "Isn't that too bad!" What that other person is really telling you is that he sees your tear but he doesn't want to get close and help. Don't waste anger training on him again because he probably doesn't care about you. Now this can be very upsetting, but if you want to maintain a relationship with that person, you may want to get help in starting some meaningful communication with him, *if* he is willing to do his part of the work.

The biggest fear of the yeller is that someone will say to her, "Hey, you have a right to be angry, but you don't have the right to abuse me!" That will really tell a yeller where she lives, and she will shrink down quickly. She was labeled the abuser that she is.

An easy way to remember the three types of anger expression (passive, aggressive, and assertive) is to visualize a person stubbing his toe on a desk corner during a meeting. The passive stuffer will hold his breath, wince with pain, and pretend it doesn't hurt. The aggressive yeller will curse out the desk and the moron who built it. To guess the assertive expresser's response, just ask any two-year-old kid to stub his toe. He'll yell, "Ouch. I just hurt my toe on that desk!" It's okay to yell (use volume) as long as it is in a self-expression instead of a projection. This means use the word "I" in your sentence first, and then say how you feel. When you start a sentence with "you" first,

97

it will usually be a critical one (projection). This is called "I language," and it is imperative for self-expression of a feeling. (Of course "you" followed by a compliment is a nurturing, positive statement.)

If you watch the movie *Pretty Woman*, you will see a scene where the main character, played by Richard Gere, describes how his father mistreated him. The character then takes a moment to rephrase his statement into I language, and then adds how much money it has cost him to be able to say that one sentence! In other words he rephrases his anger into I language. Later in the movie when he and the Julia Roberts character are having an argument, she uses "you language" and is getting more and more upset, while he continues to use I expressions and stays in control.

Poorly expressed anger (aggression, hostility) is the major cause of coronary disease as part of the Type A personality. It's literally a killer. It is also a factor in elevated cholesterol, guilt, and pain. I can't tell you how many sessions I have had with angry people whose history includes multiple bypasses.

An important element to consider is that of forgiveness. When someone is living their life allowing you to push your own button, it is wise to first forgive them (to yourself or out loud) for just being them, and then to do anger training.

It is sometimes politically or socially wise not to use anger training, but to stuff *on purpose* as a good technique in itself. As long as it is done on purpose, and not out of fear, it allows you the option not to confront an authority figure, or someone you may see as unstable.

There are other ways to deal with anger that are discussed elsewhere in this book. They include various forms of venting preventively. Too much anger turned outward will be an investment in anxiety, and too much turned inward will create depression. See the depression chapter for some of these venting techniques.

Anger training and the knowledge of how it works and why the other forms of expressing anger don't, will allow you to be genuine with your *valid* anger and let it go quickly and functionally.

Chapter 20

HIGHER-NEEDS STRESS MODEL

*J*t's really nice when life goes our way: when we have control, when people like us, when it's easy to focus on what we want, feel accepted by others, or get that feeling of high esteem when we are rewarded or recognized by our peers. In other words, it's nice to just react to good news with good feelings. That's fine when it happens, and I consider those times as little miracles.

Let's look at good news, bad news, and reacting. A reaction is automatic, done without thinking. In that way it's a facet of the ANS, as far as I'm concerned. Reacting is fine for good news, but deadly for bad news in terms of stress.

HOW TO MAKE WORRY WORK FOR YOU

If I told you that you just won the lottery, I'd hope that you would react with "Yippie, yippie, yippie!" But if I told you that your car just got towed away, I'd hate to see you just react with "Oh my God! I can't believe this! Oh, rats!" This poorly expressed reaction would hurt, leading to further stress and anger. We know from the Two Rock Stress Model that you could express your emotions ("I hate when this happens!") and then go about solving your problem, feeling the control that that brings.

The higher-needs stress model developed from psychologist Abraham Maslow by psychologist Avis K. Bennett, Ph.D., is an interesting insight into understanding your power in stress management. It allows you to take a moment *before* you react to stress to enable you to decide from among some choices on *how* to react based on the self-fulfillment of your higher needs.

Before we discuss what the higher needs are, let's first look at our basic needs and how we deal with them on a daily basis. When you are born you have certain basic needs. They include food, water, touch, warmth, and shelter. A need is not an emotion. A need gets either fulfilled or denied. When it is fulfilled, you get a positive emotion. When it is denied, you get stress and a negative emotion (anger).

Your basic needs were probably fulfilled by your mother. She fed you, kept you warm, held you, and you felt good when she did. Eventually you learned to do all those things yourself. You now meet your own basic needs daily by *self*-fulfilling them. You feed yourself, shelter yourself, and so forth. You still feel good when you do these things for yourself. Once in a while you get your basic needs fulfilled by others, as in a spa vacation. They pamper you, take care of your basic needs, and you feel terrific, like a well-cared-for baby.

It's a lifelong journey to realize your own power to self-fulfill your own higher needs. It starts at age two and keeps on going. They are the needs for control, approval, attention, affection, acceptance, and esteem. However, we fall into the trap of *expecting* these higher needs to be *externally* fulfilled, just as our basic needs were. When my higher needs get externally filled on any particular day . . . that's a miracle, for it is not life's job to fulfill these needs—it's my job!

Let's take a look at an actress who just finished

a stage performance and is receiving applause from the audience. She is receiving externally the fulfillment of most of her higher needs: acceptance, approval, esteem, affection, and attention. As a result, she also feels in control and is full of positive emotions. When the applause ends, and she is back in her dressing room, she may look in the mirror, feel angry or sad, and reach for the bottle of liquor next to her. She would do this because she cannot (will not) fulfill her own needs of *self*-acceptance, *self*-approval, *self*-esteem, *self*-affection, or *self*-attention, and thus as a result feels no *self*-control.

When we feel that kind of stress, we reach for a bad habit and inadvertently hurt the body mainly in an effort to numb the pain from a denied higher need. The actress is an example of someone who is externally oriented to the fulfillment of her own higher needs. This type of person tends to directly react to stress with more stress, bad habits, and guilt, which causes more pain. The way to break that cycle is to go internal for the need fulfillment.

See if this example helps you to understand this process better. If you're like most people, you probably suffer from occasional shoulder aches. If you observe someone with this problem, they might reach back with their hand and rub the area of discomfort while thinking to themselves, "Boy, this is killing me. I can't believe how tight this is. What a knot!" Their face would be contorted and tight while they were rubbing their shoulder. Now, if you take that same person and you go over and give them a quick massage on that shoulder, you will see their face relax, and they will be thinking or saying out loud, "Oh, that's great! Keep doing that! It feels wonderful!"

The insight here is: what is to prevent that person with the shoulder ache to reach back with their own hand and talking that nice way and letting their face relax? That is an example of self-fulfillment and self-nurturing. It's so easy but we never think about that option. It's what the body wants.

There are many things you can do when bad news reaches you that will address the higher need that is being denied. Self-fulfill it instead of reacting directly with the anger of an externally unfulfilled need. The irony is that when you rub that shoulder with the negative language and tight face, it doesn't feel any better. It probably feels worse.

If you have one or more externally developed higher-need systems they will tend to get you into trouble when you become stressed. That external need gratification keeps you from self-fulfilling. You become a stress dweller instead of a stress manager (solver).

Let's look at just a few of our higher needs that fall into the trap of expecting external fulfillment. If you're in the habit of looking for external gratification of the higher need of control, you might be that person pushing the elevator button twenty times, or cursing out the traffic jam or someone who is late for an appointment. High control people tend to be critical, judgmental, angry, impatient, intolerant, nonforgiving, angry, manipulative, yellers, angry, perfectionists, demanding, and have I mentioned angry? They have their good sides too. They are usually generous, caring, considerate, and attentive. That, of course, is when things are going their way or when they are in their post–anger and guilt stage. Anger training and understanding real control (that is, self-control) can turn their lives around, and allow them to be the special people they are.

> *The solution to being a stress dweller is that there are actions, thoughts, and feelings you can access while you are waiting for that elevator, traffic to clear, or person to arrive. That is your power. No one can take it away from you, except you. If you met a friend at that elevator while you were waiting, and had a good conversation, not only would you tend not to worry about the elevator, but you might not like it when it finally arrives because you are too deeply involved in your conversation. This is an example of the transfer of control from external to internal (self).*

A person who is an external approval need focuser would usually have trouble saying no, be a caretaker, feel unappreciated, be greatly affected by guilt, care a lot about what others thought, be passive in many of their responses to life, avoid confrontation, might use food excessively, and have difficulty receiving from others. Somehow they got stuck living other people's lives. They are responsible, hardworking, caring, sensitive, comforting people.

> *To unstick themselves they need to put self-approval first. They need to self-nurture, learn to receive graciously, say no more often when they don't want to do something, take some risks in going from passive to assertive behavior, and basically appreciate themselves. They should more readily give themselves some gifts and rub their own back with a smile.*

One example of this type of person is someone who has difficulty sending food back in a restaurant. This is passive, approval-oriented behavior. She thinks that if she made what she thinks will be a big deal about her dissatisfaction with how her food was prepared that she would lose the approval of the waiter and the other people at her table who might feel that they had to wait for her before they could start. So she'll avoid all that imagined disapproval by keeping the poorly prepared food. But what about *her* approval? However, let's look at an example of how such a situation usually plays itself out. A woman orders a steak and when asked by the waiter how it is she lies and says it's fine even though it's not. Later when he clears the table, he notices a large piece of lettuce over the steak. He pushes it aside and says, "Why didn't you tell me it wasn't done right? I could have fixed it for you." The moral: it's okay to let the waiter do his job. He wants you to keep him posted so that you'll be happy and he can get a good tip!

Someone with a highly developed need for attention usually only feels comfortable if others (external) are giving them focus and attention. A lot of people in the public eye have this need overly externalized. They usually maintain eye contact, hate interruptions, avoid call waiting or placing people on hold, and like to know that they have 100 percent of your attention. They get upset if you look at your watch or take a call while with them. These people need to develop a better sense of self-attention!

Those with high attention needs could instead focus on a good feeling, thought, plan, dream, goal, object while the other person is on the phone. They could realize that maybe you just want to know what time it is when you look at your watch, not that you're bored with them. Self-attentive children can have fun

when sent to their rooms, while external atten-
tive children will feel punished by the lack of
others' attention.

External-esteem-need people are like chame-
leons. Many times they will assume the esteem of
other people (relationships) or events (celebrations
or major disappointments). This need of theirs may
be based on an early loss of identity as a child as a
result of abandonment (physically or emotionally)
or engulfment by a powerful personality (usually
a parent). The core is empty, so the identity gets lost
when not superimposed on someone else's identity.

If that other's identity is dysfunctional (like that of
an alcoholic, controller, abuser) then the external-
need person will feel anxious or depressed or both.
If they are lucky they will link up with a person
with a functional identity that, through modeling and
nurturing acceptance, will allow their lost identity to
flourish.

High-external-esteem-need people often have
one-dimensional identities. An example of such a
person would be a workaholic stockbroker who,
at the end of the day, looks at the market results
and either feels good or bad about himself. He lets
the external market results determine his esteem for

that day. His identity is mainly associated with his work, which is summed up daily in the *Wall Street Journal*, whereas the functional internal esteem-need fulfiller (self) has many identities to fall back on when the market is experiencing a bad day. He refocuses on his solid core of self-esteem that is unaffected by what's in the *Journal*. He accepts his work identity and the ups and downs as part of the job description and not as indicators of his self-worth.

Connected closely with the esteem need is the acceptance need. A high external acceptance need will create an overcaretaker/nurturer person. This type of person is missing a self-acceptance core, which makes them sad and empty. When I see them in a session, they tend constantly to be on the verge of tears as they mourn the loss of their own experience. It is difficult to instill self-acceptance after their life (in the form of others such as parents, peers, and so forth) has convinced these people that they are not acceptable. As a result, these people practice being accepted by others on a deed-by-deed basis each day externally. It is especially painful for me to experience this type of session. Self-nurturing, self-caretaking, and self-gifts are good starting points for the long inward journey to self-fulfillment of their higher needs.

But remember: external need fulfillment is fine as long as it is secondary to the self-fulfillment of higher needs.

Chapter 21

DEPRESSION AND ITS NATURAL ENEMIES

*S*imple depression certainly comes under the range of "normal nuts" stress-related symptoms. Many of us have days when we feel down, sad, have little energy, or feel a bit empty. It might be because of an event that was a downer, or that we have too much spare time on our hands, or that we are coming down from a period of high energy. Depression could happen for no reason at all, or for something as specific as a rainy day. In any case . . . we feel a little depressed.

Psychologists tell us that depression is anger turned inward. We stuff our feelings of anger and get depressed to some degree. Many times we have difficulty determining the origin of that anger. It could be recent or very old stuff. I'd like to offer some successful solutions to this simple depression:

1. *Vent Your Anger*—To deal better with the anger origin of simple depression, it is essential to create a way of venting that anger. The object is to get the anger out. If you are aware of what the anger is about, you could vent it by writing in a journal, by talking about it to your friends, or by discussing it in therapy. These are all good, traditional ways to express anger and thus vent it. Sometimes you don't have a good handle on the specifics of the anger. I'd like to suggest a powerful and sometimes frightening (read exciting!) approach to venting anger. I call this method the "dysfunctional vent."

Imagine you are a cave person in the early days of man. You're in your "cave sweet cave" and your spouse is inventing the wheel. Since your spouse is of limited intelligence the wheel is in the shape of a square. Your spouse "rolls" the wheel over to show you how well it works and it thumps (it's made of rock) on your foot, breaking every bone. How do you feel? What do you feel like doing to your spouse? (Remember, back then there were no lawyers or death penalty.) The correct answer is that you'd like to "club" that spouse into next week!

Anger is the main response to stress. Many have called it the stress emotion. The indirect way we are going to get at this anger (known or unknown) is through a variation of a movement therapy technique. Movement therapy is an unknown healing art to many, and is greatly misunderstood by many more. It's hard to describe, so I'm only going to give you a definition from my point of view. To me, it works in a body-mind direction. You get the body moving a certain way (that is, facilitated by a movement therapist) and then you look into your feelings and thoughts. With anger, for example, you might have the client hit a pillow with their fist and see what feelings and words surface. I believe if you hit a pillow long enough, it begins to take on the appearance of people who are close to you (Mom, Dad, . . . that idiot I married!).

The following description of my dysfunctional vent approach modifies the pillow-beating approach a bit. I call it dysfunctional as opposed to the functional methods of venting already mentioned, such as journal writing, therapy, and so forth.

Start off by going into your bathroom and closing the door. Face the mirror and have a clock in front of you to tell you when three minutes are up. Start with a really bloodcurdling scream: you want *rage* here. You want to almost scare yourself. Now you're on your way to getting angry. Take these three minutes to be totally external about everything in your life. Blame, bitch, complain, moan, groan, yell, abuse the world, and get busy doing it. Don't be nice. This is a projection festival with the volume turned up to 11 (in *Spinal Tap* terms). Rant and rave. Get it out. Don't be afraid. It's just an exercise to vent the most direct way without actually hurting others. You just want to test-drive your rage a little.

If your deepest fear is that you could actually kill someone, do this with the aid of a therapist first. When the clock tells you that your time is up, cool down and feel the sense of release the venting gave you. Later that day your throat might hurt a little. You're not getting a cold, it was from all the yelling. You managed to release some anger, if not *the* anger, and it's made you feel a little better and more in control.

2. *Endorphin Exercise*—Daily aerobic exercise followed by a twenty-minute "endorphin appreciation" as outlined in the maximizing exercise chapter

will act as a natural antidepressant as well as produce more white blood cells, which also deter depression and bolster the immune system.

3. *Change the Script*—Biofeedback as well as cognitive psychology (how we talk to ourselves and the feelings that are elicited from those words) have shown us that changing the way we think, or changing the script, moments before a depressing feeling can have quick, powerful results. When a depressing feeling starts to hit, be prepared with some uplifting "scripts" that produce good adrenaline, instead of simply trying to relax. Try this risky, uplifting thinking and feel the aliveness come over you. For me, that's the best antidote to depression: living, not sedating with relaxation.

In a 1940s movie called *Apartment for Peggy*, there's an old man who is considering suicide and asks Peggy (a real optimist) for her advice. She says, "What good would dying do? You're already dead! You need LIFE!" That's the ticket! The E-ticket. An E-ticket is the ticket you buy at an amusement park that covers all the rides. We all need more living in our life. Our depressing scripts could really use pumping up with good adrenaline.

Since it's fantasy and in the privacy of your own mind, why not see the effect this good adrenaline has on your body. It will usually put a smile on your face. Just write a new script with your mind and let the good adrenaline do its work.

4. *Have a Functional Depression*—To some extent depression can be defined as depressed energy. In numbers, it's as though you're at 12 but you want to be at 20. You can only do the 12 stuff but feel depressed that you can't do the full 20. If you can create a plan to *use* the 12 instead of trying (read failing) to get to 20, you will gain a slight feeling of control over the 12 that you have. As far as I'm concerned, the attempt to do 20 only adds to your depressed state. Having what is called a functional depression is being able to use that 12 in a positive way. For instance, resting, getting away from it all, avoiding decisions, taking care of your body, expressing your feelings directly or through an art form (writing, painting, and so forth), looking for a lesson, and becoming self-aware. Many artists create special works during their blue periods that probably reflect some of that lowered energy or depression. Have a good 12!

5. *Just Do It!*—Finally, I see simple depression as the ultimate in procrastination. Deep down we know that engagement with life is the best prescription for depression. One client that I was seeing for depression hadn't been in for a few weeks. When I called him he told me he didn't have time to see me right now because he was too busy doing stuff. He had found living.

We all have those moments of living—we just need to put them all in a row and have a functional life! One way to make this happen is to use a technique involving the doing stage from the chapter on procrastination. Here's how it works:

> *During a moment when you are feeling a little up rather than depressed, make a list of things you like or love to do that are available and doable in your home or area. Label the list "activities." Above that write the words "this won't work!" and at the bottom of the list write "five minutes." The next time you feel depressed, empty, sad, low energy, go to this list, look over the many activities that you could do and say the words you are thinking: "This won't work!" You won't want to do these items now because your ANS is playing*

a trick on you. The words on the top are to remind you of that trap! Pick one activity and just do it for five minutes and see if you don't feel better, more alive—you're living. This five-minute "soak time" allows you to get lost in living just as that client of mine did. You'll be too busy doing to feel depressed over not doing.

Chapter 22

SAYING NO—IT'S ABOUT TIME

A complaint I hear often is, "I'm always rushing. There's never enough time. I can't get it all done. I just don't have the time." Almost always this feeling is a result of not saying no enough at work, at home, and in relationships.

To buy a yes for you, you need to spend a no on someone else. Part of the difficulty in saying no is that it is incorrectly linked to external approval. Priorities are arranged to put yourself last so you won't offend anyone. But what about you? You count! The confusion here is that you believe the approval need connection and create a catch-22 no-win situation for yourself. If you see it for what it really is (a control connection), you will put your-self into a no-lose position.

Let's take the approval connection first and see why it makes you fail at saying no.

You're probably a very nice person. If you were wearing a T-shirt the message on the front would be "I'm a nice person." The message on the back, the one you can't see, is the real message. It says, "I need to be liked." When someone asks you to do something or for a favor, you will usually say yes because you're a nice person (you need to be liked). You will help that person and say yes. You may not have wanted to do that favor so now you feel stuck doing something you don't like. If you'd said no, you wouldn't be that nice person, and you think they wouldn't like you, and that would make you feel bad as well. That's the catch-22 of this approval connection scenario.

If your best friend asked you for a favor, then saw you look briefly at your watch and sigh a little breath, she might say to you, "Oh, you can't really do it, it's okay." She would let you off the hook. She would say that no for you by reading your mind (body language actually). Unfortunately, that doesn't happen enough and others are more than

CRAIG B. MARDUS, PH.D.

happy to let you say yes and do their work for them. That's why it's important to say that no clearly for yourself.

Now let's look at the control connection of saying no and see how it is a no-lose scenario.

> *When someone asks you for a favor, or to do something you don't have to do as part of your job, you have the right to say no. It's really about* control. *When you say no, you are saying that you don't want to fix (control) their problem, but instead are giving it back to them (for their control to deal with). It's like playing tennis. You are saying, "No, thanks, it's back in your court."*

Let's look at an example of both approval and control in saying no. If a manipulative person (friend, relative, co-worker) asks you for a favor ("Do this for me?") and you reply with a timid no, he might say, "Why not? Why can't you do it?" He is looking for your excuse. The only excuse that kind of person will accept is if you are going for chemotherapy that afternoon! He still might ask you to do it on your way back! People like him will make you feel bad about saying no, and you have indeed lost their approval. The interesting thing about them is that you never really had their approval, you only had it when doing their favors. That's what we call a fair-weather friend.

If a functional (not manipulative) person asks you for a favor, and you say no, she will think or say out loud something like, "Oh, that's all right. I think I can get someone else to take care of it or maybe I can get to it later." You'll actually see her take the *control* of the problem back (in their court) and start dealing with it (control) instead of asking you for excuses. She didn't take it personally or as an approval issue. She (functionally) took it as the shift of control that it was really about.

With this knowledge you can make a no easier on yourself if, when you say no, you add something like this, "But I'm sure you'll find a way of getting it done." That lets the other person know it is about control and not approval.

The way this works either way (no lose) is that when you say no with that additional phrase, you will get one of two responses: 1) The person functionally receives the no and

*shows the person is going to solve it himself
and honors your decision. This buys a yes for
you, and you feel okay. That's a win for you.
2) The person doesn't honor your no, asks
for your excuse, withdraws his approval, and
metaphorically hands you a card that says,
"I'm a fair-weather friend and just tried to use
you!" That's also a win for you because you
can't lose approval from someone who never
really gave it.*

It's important to acknowledge one thing before
you begin to use this approach. Your past reputa-
tion as a yes-sayer needs to be cleared. Talk to your
friends, family, and co-workers when they are in
a good mood. *Tell* them that you need to make
better use of your time so you will be saying no in
the future to some of their requests. Also, this is a
good time to apologize for allowing yourself to do
favors, errands, tasks in the past that you really
didn't want to do. You need to reclaim time now,
and you hope they will understand your future nos.

Explaining yourself this way is an important step
and sets the scene for the future. It will not shock
them this way. You might also tell them you will

be asking more favors of them in the future. Check out the looks you get with that one!

One client summed up a session on saying no beautifully. As a former yes-sayer to favors and extra work, he considered himself a can-do guy at work. Now he considers himself a can-do-less guy!

Chapter 23

INSTANT SELF-ESTEEM

$\mathcal{J}$ believe that self-esteem isn't something you have, rather it's something you believe . . . NOW. It's easy to see how well you think and feel about yourself when others praise or reward you (external). If that kind of high esteem can be felt that strongly from just a mere outside praise, then think how easy it would be to give it from the inside! You're already in there. The important thing here is to understand that it is easy and that it is demonstrated every time you are complimented. Your autonomic nervous system is telling you something about how it works. Whether you make use of this ease of attaining your own *self*-esteem or not is up to you . . . NOW.

You can blame your parents, childhood, bad luck, or the stars but the bottom line is: what is it going to take to start treating yourself with care? The moment you do, you will feel instant self-esteem! Read your résumé of positive qualities to yourself and give yourself permission to believe them . . . NOW.

You have two inner parents: a critical one and a nurturing one. Switch away from the critical one and allow access to the nurturing one. It's an attitude shift that will change your life. You have a core of many identities. You are ruler of your core. No one can touch it unless you let them access your critical parent within. That's the henchman who does the dirty work. When one of your identities (worker, wife, husband, son, daughter) makes a human error (mistake), forgive and nurture yourself, and feel good about the lucky day your other identities had! Call in your other identities as "back-up." Be a kinder, gentler ruler of your core.

An attitude is hard to change because most of us don't even know we have one. An attitude is like a heavy accent. We can't tell we have one, but it is overwhelmingly obvious to everyone else!

One of the shortest sessions I ever had was with a client who taught me a lesson I shall cherish forever. When I asked him how he saw life, he compared it to a game of tennis. He said that no matter how much spin (dysfunction) your opponent (people, life) puts on the ball, your job is to hit it back straight and true (function). You'll be tempted to put your own spin on it, but that will only hurt you. Play from within and don't be influenced by another's spin. For you, your best game is straight and true. You can trust it and learn from it. I say it was a short session because he needed no work. He gave me a session.

Chapter 24

LIFE *IS* A DREAM!

$\mathcal{F}$or me the best way to get along with life is to see it the same way you see dreams.

If you had a strange dream and went to a therapist to analyze it, it would be apparent that you were the only real person in the dream. All the other people, things, monsters, aliens, talking hot dogs were figments of your imagination. The analysis would take the form of finding out the meaning for you, the only real person. You wouldn't spend your hard-earned money trying to fix or help a character in your dream! Then you would really need a therapist! All the characters are merely putting on a play to teach you about an aspect of yourself. They are all part of you.

CRAIG B. MARDUS, PH.D.

Who's to know if life really isn't a dream within
a dream? When you try to fix or help other people
in life, you're missing the point of the dream. You
were meant to come in contact with these people
and events (family, friends, co-workers, disasters)
to learn about yourself. Don't waste your life
(dream) fixing the other players—they're only
there to teach you about you. That's when you
have the power to change yourself and accept them.

See life, the world, stress, bad luck, trauma, others' abusiveness as a part of your dream. You will
survive with the right attitude (seeing the dream as
only a drama with a lesson for you, *if* you can allow
yourself to see the lesson instead of getting stressed
by the drama).

Even this book is not real. It's part of your
dream. You were meant to dream it so you could
change yourself through its insight. Or you could
just chalk it up as "some crazy dream" that doesn't
mean anything.

The ball's in your court . . .